Bible Phonics
Workbook 1

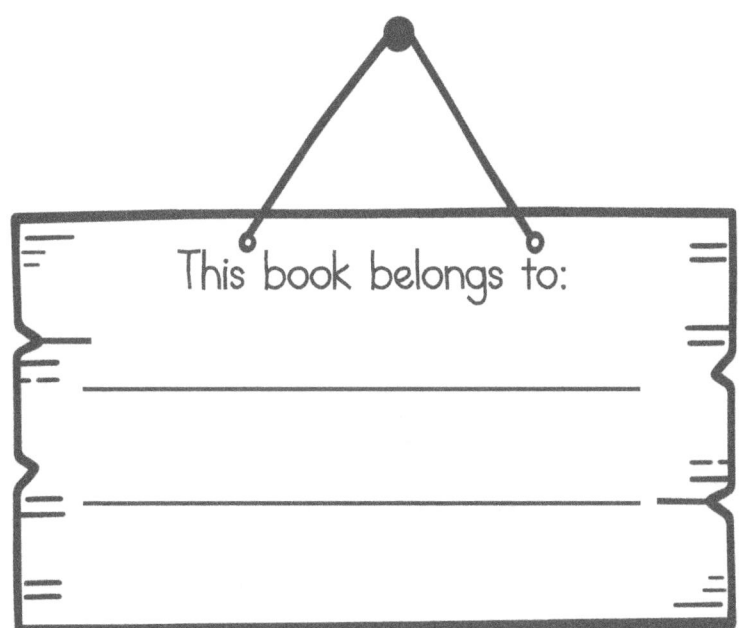

This book belongs to:

Quail Publishers

About the Series

Quail Publishers' Bible Phonics series is a revised version of the Success with Phonics series. The series includes comprehensive, high quality, Bible-based products that are aligned to English language K-2 standards. The program utilizes the Science of Reading components: phonemic awareness, phonics, vocabulary, fluency, and comprehension, to ensure literacy. The explicit, systematic phonics strategies get children reading and writing from an early age, while promoting Bible principles and teachings. Each book covers a group of the most common sound-spelling combinations of the English language, with engaging, multi-sensory activities for children to read fluently and confidently.

Quail Publishers grants teachers permission to photocopy the designated reproducible pages from this book for classroom use. No other part of this publication may be reproduced, stored in a retrieval system or transmitted in any form or by any means, electronic, mechanical, photocopying, recording or otherwise, without the prior permission of the publisher.

Written by Allison Hall. Edited by Keisha Baboolal and Myrtle Hall
Interior design by Allison Hall
Bible Illustrations by Wayne Powell
Other illustrations sourced from Pixabay, Dreamstime and FreePik. Used under license.
Bible verses adapted from the Authorized King James Version
Text Copyright © 2023 by Allison Hall
All rights reserved. Published by Quail Publishers LLC
Coral Springs, Florida USA
Email: info@quailpublishers.com or quailpublishers@gmail.com
Website: www.quailpublishers.com

ISBN: 978-0-9894627-7-8

Table of Contents

Introduction	4
Handwriting	9
The /S/ sound	10
The /A/ sound	12
The /T/ sound	14
The /P/ sound	16
Review of the Sounds	18
The /I/ sound	19
The /N/ sound	21
The /M/ sound	23
The /D/ sound	25
High Frequency Word (is)	27
High Frequency Word (as)	28
Blending, Spelling Reading	29
The /G/ sound	30
The /O/ sound	32
The /C/ sound	34
The /K/ sound	36
Blending, Spelling Reading	38
The /CK/ sound	39
High Frequency Word (I)	40
Reviewing Sounds	41
Rhymes	42
Building Words, Word Families	43
Steps to Spelling	44
High Frequency Word (and)	45
The Alphabet	46
Comprehension	47
Building Sentences	48
Reading	49
Numbers and their names	50
Word List	51
Letter Tiles	52

Introduction

Bible Phonics™ is an engaging, explicit and systematic approach to teach phonics, integrated with Bible teachings, concepts, and themes. In Bible Phonics™ A-B-C, the first book in the series, children were taught alphabetic recognition skills. However, in the second series of Bible Phonics™ workbooks, the letters are not taught in alphabetic order. The letters, **s**, **a**, **t**, and **p**, are introduced first. This phoneme sequence is used in many English-speaking countries, as it allows children to build and read words quickly and easily. Using this sequence, children can build the words: **at**, **sat**, **pat**, **tap** and **sap**, with the first four letters. Each letter is introduced with a connected Bible story to foster Bible knowledge and as reinforcement. High frequency words with irregular spelling patterns are also taught, using the **Read-Spell-Write** strategy.

TEACHING WITH THE ACTIVITY SHEETS

Bible Phonics™ is suitable for Christian schools, churches and homes. The workbooks fully complement the kindergarten and children's Bible class curriculums. There are two reproducible pages dedicated to teaching each letter sound and its connected Bible lesson. There are also activities to help you review the sounds taught. When children participate in the multisensory activities in the books, they learn:

- **Bible Teachings:** Learn about Christ's teachings, life in ancient Israel and more
- **Phonemic Awareness**: Identify sounds in spoken words
- **Phonics:** Understand letter-sound correspondences
- **Handwriting**: Write the letters and letter combinations that represent each sound
- **Spelling**:
    * Use picture clues to complete words with the target sound
    * Identify the correct spelling of words with the target sound
- **Reading**: Read decodable sentences with words with the target sound
- **Composition:** Build sentences with the target sound
- **Comprehension**: Read decodable stories and rhymes

The pace of each lesson is always dependent on children's mastery of each letter sound and understanding of the lesson. Children should also fully understand a letter sound, before another is introduced.

Using the Bible to Teach Phonics

Before the Lesson

1. Review all aspects of the letter and main picture you will be teaching.

2. Read the Bible story, or connected text, and further literature on phonics.

3. Develop an exciting and engaging lesson which allows for multisensory activities and integrate technology, where applicable.

4. Make sure that children have the necessary stationery and resources to participate in the lesson.

5. Ensure lessons have activities to foster home-school connection.

6. Be aware that some children will have more advanced phonics knowledge than others. Use differentiated instruction to meet each student's needs.

Teaching the Lesson

7a. **Alphabet Recognition** – Make sure that students have alphabet recognition and phonemic awareness skills.

7b. **Phonemic Awareness – Invite children to listen carefully as you say the sound you are teaching. Precise pronunciation, or pure sounds, should be said for all letters.** Slide the sound into the picture name. For example say, /ssssnake/. Always, stress the sound you are teaching and model the proper mouth position to say each letter sound correctly. Ask children to repeat the sound thrice. Invite them to name the letter that says the sound.

Note that some sounds are continuous and can be easily stretched (stretchy sounds), for example /sss/. However some are non-continuous sounds and can't be stretched (bouncy sounds), for example /ă/. Non-continuous sounds must be said at least thrice, so that children hear them clearly. Children should also be made aware that a sound can be represented by two letters, for example 'ch' stand for /ch/. This is called a digraph, however in a consonant blend such as **c/l**, both sounds are heard. Children should be taught to sound out the digraph, not the sounds of the individual letters.

8. **Phonics - Inform children that every letter has a name and a shape, and stands for a sound, or sounds. For example, letter 's' stands for /s/, as in snake. Draw their attention to the supporting main picture in their workbooks.** If there is a child in the class with a name that begins with the letter and sound you are teaching, say his/her name. For example, say, "/s/ also stands for **S**am". Briefly discuss aspects of the main picture. For example, some snakes make a hissing sound that says /sss/. Their bodies can also form an 's' shape when they slither or crawl.

9. **Letter Formation - Write the letter in its upper and lower case forms on the board.** Show the sequence in which each letter is formed and the proper pencil grip. Have children use the activity sheets to write the letters properly, and develop beautiful and legible handwriting.

Use mnemonics where necessary. For example, for letter 's', you can say, "Make it look like a snake. Curve to the left, then curve to the right". Point out to children that letters look alike and have various shapes or font styles. For example: 'b' and 'd' are often confused.

10. **Letter Knowledge - Inform children that letter sounds can be heard at the beginning, middle and end of words.** The activities in the book allow children to further build their letter knowledge. Always read and explain the instructions to children.

11. **Reading Connection - Read a Bible story relating to each main picture to promote reading, Bible knowledge,** a sense of story, comprehension skills, and as reinforcement strategies. Ask students questions about each story. There are also sentences and short passages that children must read to apply, practice and master their phonics skills. Students should also be engaged in other interesting multicultural literature daily.

12. **Blending – As soon as children have learned the first three letters, they should be taught to blend letter sounds to read words with vowel-consonant (VC), and consonant-vowel-consonant (CVC) phonemes.** These are popularly called green words, as they are phonetically decodable. The green symbolizes 'go', as children should read them easily. Use onsets and rimes (word families) to help children to read and spell these words quickly.

13. **Writing – Once children have learned a number of words, you should guide them in spelling, reading, and composing simple sentences.** Reinforce that a sentence starts with a capital letter and has an end mark.

14. **Reinforcement – Use songs, puppets, art and craft, and other activities to make the lessons more engaging and meaningful, integrate subject areas, and reinforce the letter and sound being taught.** Revise the letters of alphabet in sequence often.

15. **Assessment** – Use authentic assessment tools to measure students' progress

Blending Words

Blending is a very important phonics skill that children must master to read words and build fluency. Blending is the first stage in reading as letters are no longer seen in isolation. It involves sliding the individual speech sounds (phonemes) in a word quickly, in order to decode the word. Mastery of blending words improves with modeling and practice. Always model the blending process and reinforce the procedures. Here are some steps to take when blending a word.
1. Write the word '**at**' on the board. Place sound buttons or dots (•) under the letters in the words. Sound buttons tell children how many phonemes are in a word. To indicate a digraph or trigraph, a line is used.
2. Point to the letter '**a**' and invite the children to say its sound. Then point to letter '**t**' and invite the children to say its sound.
2. Sound talk the word while slowly sliding your finger under it. Sound talk is saying the sounds in the word slowly, only leaving a short gap between words. Say, **a→t**.
3. Do the procedure again quickly and say the word /**at**/. Avoid pausing between sounds. Invite students to say the word. Ask them how many sounds are in the word. Always explain the meaning of unfamiliar words.
4. Add the letter '**s**' at the beginning of the word, then invite children to say the new word. Place new words on the word wall. Then inform children to place it in their word bank.
5. Provide opportunities for children to work as partners to spell green words, using onsets and rimes (word families). This can be done with letter cards or tiles.

High Frequency Words

High frequency words are those words that appear most frequently in texts. These words include, '**and**', '**I**', '**is**', '**the**', '**can**' and '**to**'. Children must learn these words very early in order to read sentences automatically, accurately and fluently. Some high frequency words can be decoded easily, as they follow the regular spelling rules. However, some have tricky parts that do not follow the regular spelling rules and can be a challenge for young readers. These irregular spelled words are called sight words or tricky words or red words, as it is expected that children should *read them when they see them*. There are also some words, such as '**her**' and '**like**', that do not have an irregular spelling pattern. However, they can be taught as sight words, as children may not yet be introduced to their sounds and spellings.

Teaching Sight Words

The Bible Phonics™ program uses the Read-Write-Spell strategy to teach sight or tricky words. Here some steps to teach sight words using this strategy.

- Say the sight word being taught three times. Ask children to repeat the word twice.

- Invite children to sound out the letters in the word.

- Discuss the irregular, or tricky part of the word (*where the letter does not correspond to the sound, or sounds children associate with that letter*). For example, letter 's' <u>can</u> stand for /z/ in words.

- Have children trace the word, after which they will spell the word on their own.

- Write the sight word on a card and place it on a word wall. Color-code the word, to remind children of the tricky part. Children should write it in their word bank.

- Refer to the word regularly until children learn it.

Reinforcement Strategies

Word Wall
A word wall is a great tool that supports phonics instruction. It is a display of words, or word parts, that is used to teach spelling, reading and writing. Mount words with the sound-spelling being taught or sight words on a wall as reinforcement.

Word Bank
A word bank is a great way for children to improve their vocabulary, create a word list, reinforce alphabetical order and memorize the spelling of unfamiliar words. Children may use a notebook to create their word banks. Have them devote a sheet of paper for each letter. At the top of each page, they should write each letter in its upper and lower-case forms. Ensure that they start with letters '**Aa**', as the bank should be arranged in alphabetical order. Children should place new words they have learned in their bank.

Name _____   Date _____

Alphabet Recognition: Sing the alphabet song. Then touch each letter and say the initial sound it stands for.

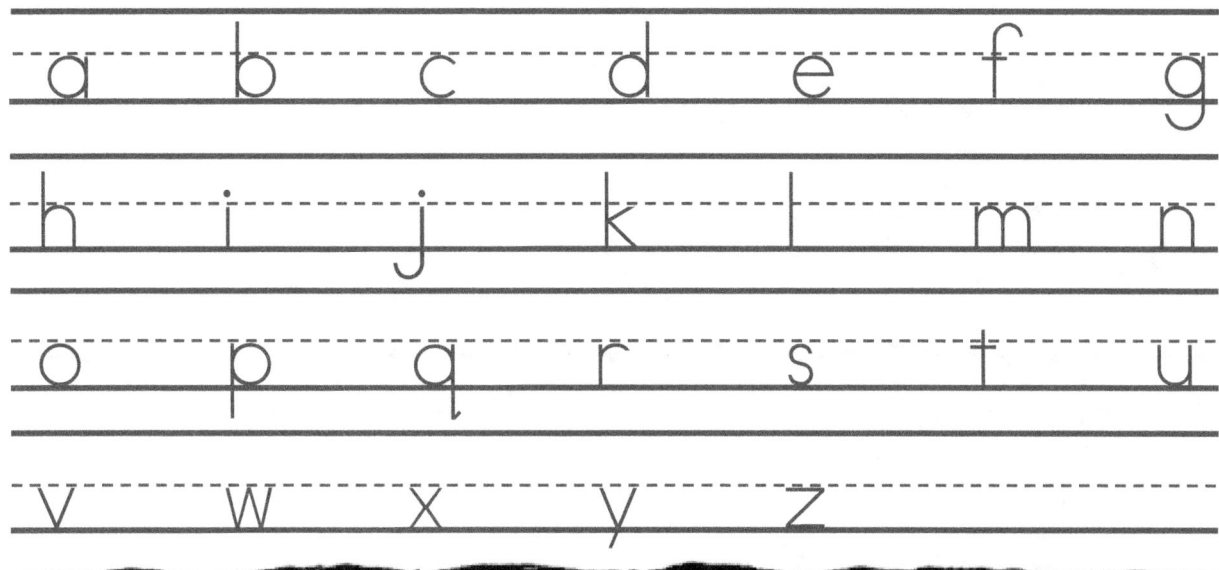

Prewriting Skills: The lines below form the foundation of our letter shapes. Trace the lines. Practice writing them in your note book.

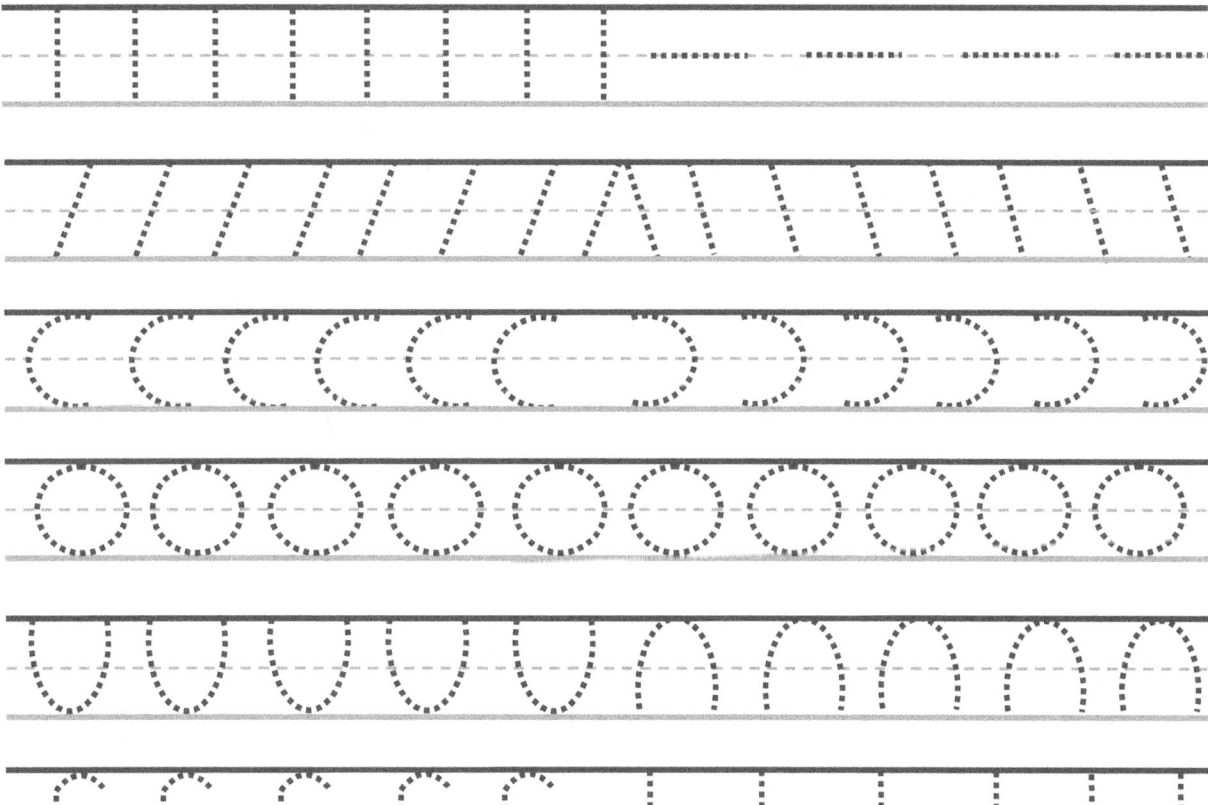

© Quail Publishers LLC 2023

Name _____   Date _____

The /s/ Sound
Say the picture name. Listen for the **first** letter sound. Say the sound.

Ss  **s**nake

---

Story Time: Listen carefully as your teacher or parent reads the Bible story below. What did you learn from the story?

Bible Story: Satan the Sly Snake
Bible Lesson: Genesis 3:1-24
Bible Theme: Obey God

Adam and Eve were the first people on earth. God placed them in the beautiful Garden of Eden. He told them to take care of the plants and animals in it. God told them to eat fruits from all the trees, except those from the Tree of Knowledge of Good and Evil. God also told them not to touch it, or they would die.

One day Satan the evil angel came into the Garden. He had changed himself to look like a snake.

"Sssssss," said the sly snake. "Did God tell you not to eat from this tree?" Eve told Satan what God had said. But Satan told her that if she ate from the tree, she would be like God. Eve wanted to be like God, so she picked a fruit from the tree and ate it. She then gave some to Adam.

Adam and Eve soon found out that they were tricked. They were naked and afraid, so they ran and hid in the bushes. God put them out of the Garden of Eden and punished Satan.

Adam and Eve lost their beautiful home, because they did not obey God. **We must always obey God.**

Name _____ Date _____

Handwriting
Trace and write.

Spelling
Say the name of each picture. Then write the missing letters to complete the words.

__un   ba__ket   bu__

Identifying Sounds
Say the name of each picture. Then circle those that **begin** with the sound /s/.

Bible Phonics Workbook 1 | 11

Name _____   Date _____

The /ă/ Sound

Say the picture name. Listen for the **first** letter sound. Say the sound. It is the short 'a' sound.

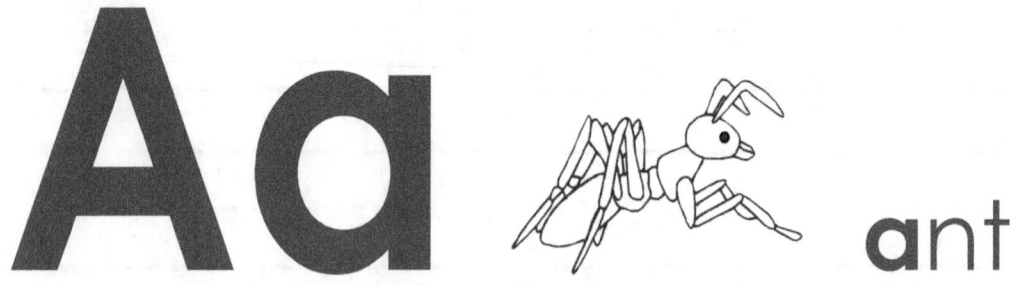 ant

Story Time: Listen carefully as your teacher or parent reads the Bible story below. What did you learn from the story?

Bible Story: Amazing Ant
Bible Lesson: Proverbs 6:6
Bible Theme: Be Wise

Did you know that ants are very wise animals? The Bible says that lazy people should follow the ant. This will make them wise.

Ants are wise because they are hardworking, strong, and love to work together. Ants also love to build, plant, share, and save. The ant's wise ways have been told in many stories, such as The Ant and the Grasshopper.

Ants are insects. They live together in a big family. The ant family is led by a queen. The queen is the only ant that can lay eggs. The queen and the males are the only ones with wings.

Ants are indeed amazing animals. **We should all follow the ant and be wise.**

Name _____   Date _____

Handwriting
Trace and write.

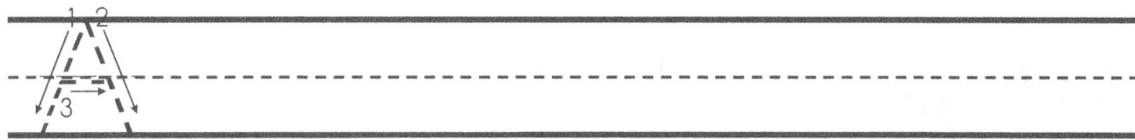

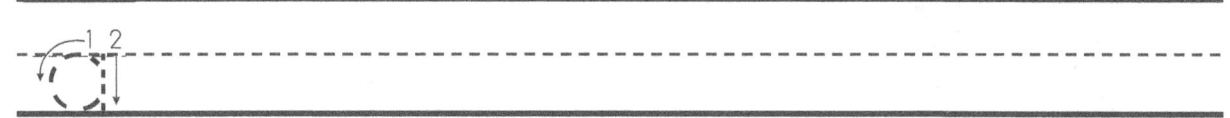

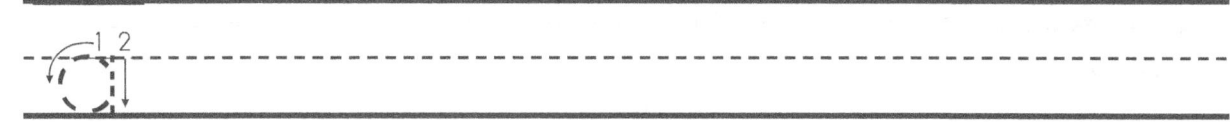

Spelling
Say the name of each picture. Then write the missing letters to complete the words.

__rrow   b__g   umbrell__

Identifying Sounds
Say the name of each picture. Then circle those that **begin** with the sound /ă/.

Name _____   Date _____

The /t/ Sound

Say the picture name. Listen for the **first** letter sound. Say the sound.

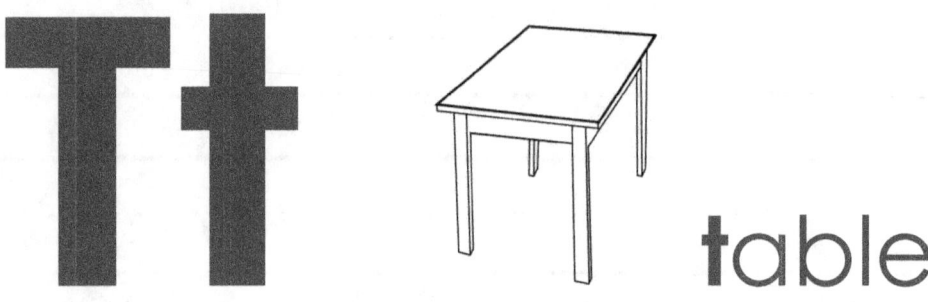

table

Story Time: Listen carefully as your teacher or parent reads the Bible story below. What did you learn from the story?

Bible Story: Jesus Tosses the Tables
Bible Lesson: Mark 11:15-18
Bible Theme: Respect God's House

Jesus loved to worship in the temple. He went there very often when he was on earth.

One day, while he was in Jerusalem, he visited the temple. There were people buying and selling animals in the temple. Jesus did not like what they were doing.

Jesus turned over the tables in the temple. He drove the animals out of the temple. Jesus also drove out the buyers and sellers. He stopped other people, who wanted to carry things through the temple courtyard.

"My house is a House of Prayer for everyone," Jesus said. "But you have made it into a place for thieves." This made the priests and teachers very angry, **but Jesus wants us to respect God's house.**

Name _____   Date _____

Handwriting
Trace and write.

Spelling
Say the name of each picture. Then write the missing letters to complete the words.

__urtle   cur__ain   ba__

Identifying Sounds
Say the name of each picture. Then circle those that **begin** with the sound /t/.

Name _____   Date _____

The /p/ Sound

Say the picture name. Listen for the **first** letter sound. Say the sound.

Story Time: Listen carefully as your teacher or parent reads the Bible story below. What did you learn from the story?

Bible Story: The Pigs Plunge
Bible Lesson: Mark 5:1-20
Bible Theme: Jesus Cleanses

A man with an unclean spirit lived in the tombs of a village. The spirit made the man very sick. He would hurt himself and cry out. The villagers often chained him, but he would pull the chains and run away.

One day Jesus visited the village. When the man saw Jesus, he ran towards him.

The man then fell on his knees and cried out, "What do you want from me Jesus, Son of the Most High God? Do not punish me!"

Jesus said, "Come out of the man you unclean spirit!" But there were many spirits in the man. The spirits begged Jesus not to send them out of the country. They asked him to go into some pigs nearby.

Jesus sent the spirits into the pigs. The pigs ran wildly and jumped over a cliff. They fell into the sea and drowned. The man was happy to be better. **He thanked Jesus and told everyone that Jesus healed him and made him clean.**

Name _____ Date _____

Handwriting
Trace and write.

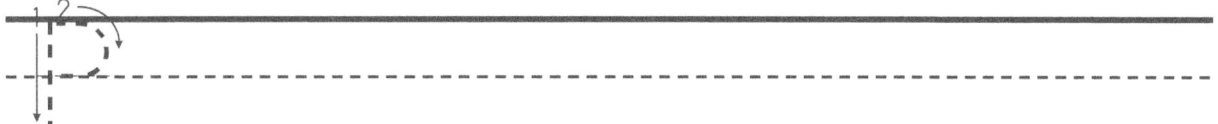

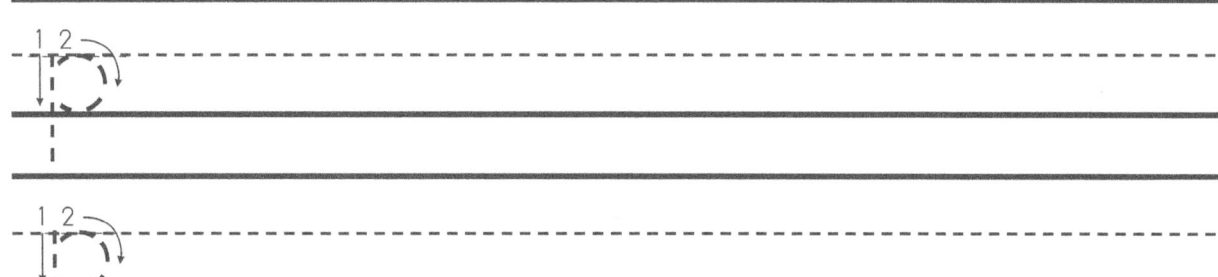

Spelling
Say the name of each picture. Then write the missing letters to complete the words.

__encil   a__ron   ca__

Identifying Sounds
Say the name of each picture. Then circle those that **begin** with the sound /p/.

Name _____ Date _____

Blending
Use sound talk to say the letter sounds in each word. Then blend the sounds to read the words.

at   sat   pat

tap   sap   pap

Spelling
Say the picture names. Then circle the correct spelling that represents each picture.

tap sap   sap tap   pat sat

Reading
Read the caption.

At a tap.

Name _____   Date _____

The /ĭ/ Sound

Say the picture name. Listen for the **first** letter sound. Say the sound. It is the short 'i' sound.

Ii 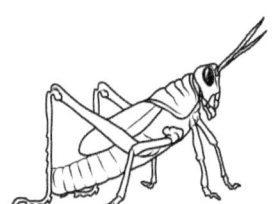 insect

Story Time: Listen carefully as your teacher or parent reads the Bible story below. What did you learn from the story?

> **Bible Story**: Icky Insects
> **Bible Lesson**: Exodus 10:1-20
> **Bible Theme**: Obey God

Pharaoh, the King of Egypt, did not want the Israelites to leave his country.

God told Moses to tell Pharaoh, "Let my people go so that they can worship me." But Pharaoh was stubborn. He wanted the Israelites to continue to work as slaves.

God punished the Egyptians. Still, Pharaoh did not let the Israelites leave.

God said to Moses, "Stretch out your hand over Egypt. I will let locusts come into the land."

A locust is a type of grasshopper. The icky insects ate all the plants. The Egyptians did not have enough to eat. They were hungry and angry. Pharaoh begged Moses to ask God to stop punishing them.

Shortly after, God sent the insects away. But Pharaoh still did not free the Israelites. God punished the Egyptians even more. Afterward, Pharaoh let the Israelites go to their new land. **We must always obey God.**

Name _____   Date _____

Handwriting
Trace and write.

Spelling
Say the name of each picture. Then write the missing letters to complete the words.

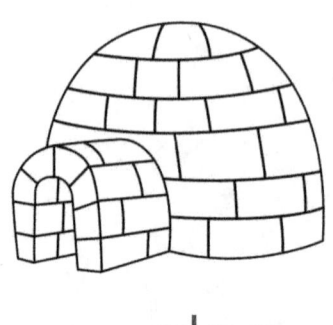      

___gloo   b___n   f___sh

Identifying Sounds
Say the name of each picture. Then circle those that **begin** with the sound /ĭ/.

Name _____   Date _____

The /n/ Sound

Say the picture name. Listen for the **first** letter sound. Say the sound.

Nn  nail

Story Time: Listen carefully as your teacher or parent reads the Bible story below. What did you learn from the story?

Bible Story: The Nail Prints
Bible Lesson: John 20:19-29
Bible Theme: Believe in Jesus

One Sunday evening Jesus appeared and stood among his disciples. Jesus had just come back to life and the disciples were hiding in a house, as they were afraid of the Jewish leaders. The disciples were very happy to see Jesus.

Thomas, one of the disciples, was not there when Jesus came by. When the others told Thomas that they had seen Jesus, he did not believe.

Thomas said, "If I do not see the holes in his hands or put my fingers in the holes in his palms and side, I will not believe."

When they killed Jesus, the big, sharp nails made holes in his hands and side. This was what Thomas wanted to see.

Eight days later, Jesus visited his disciples again. The doors in the room were shut. Suddenly, Jesus appeared. Thomas was there. Jesus told Thomas to put his finger in the holes in his hands and side. Thomas did what Jesus asked. He then cried out, "My Lord and God!"

Jesus said to Thomas, "You believe because you see me. But many people will not see me and still believe in me." **We must always believe in Jesus.**

Name _____   Date _____

Handwriting
Trace and write.

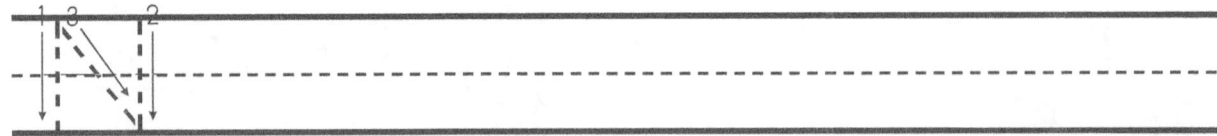

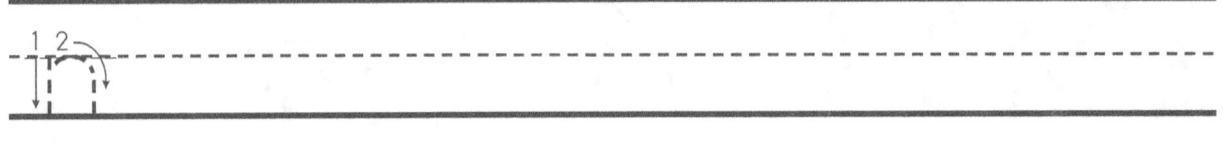

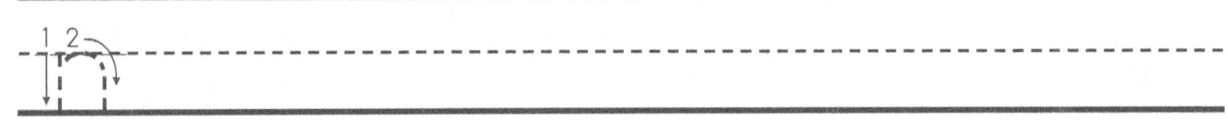

Spelling
Say the name of each picture. Then write the missing letters to complete the words.

__est   pe__cil   pa__

Identifying Sounds
Say the name of each picture. Then circle those that **begin** with the sound /n/.

Name _____   Date _____

The /m/ Sound

Say the picture name. Listen for the **first** letter sound. Say the sound.

Mm  moon

---

Story Time: Listen carefully as your teacher or parent reads the Bible story below. What did you learn from the story?

Bible Story: Marvelous Moon
Bible Lesson: Romans 12:1
Bible Theme: Believe in Jesus

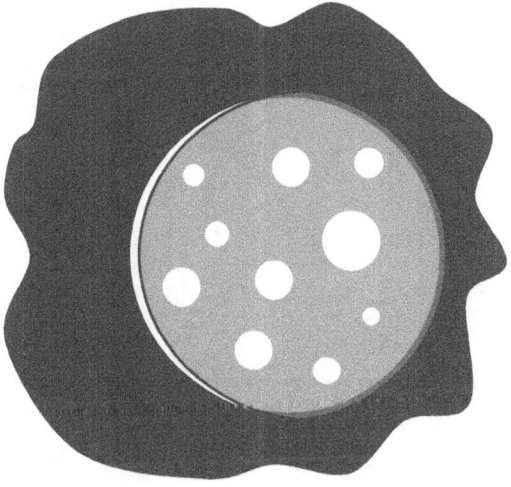

God made the moon on the fourth day of creation. The moon gives us light at night. It gets its light from the sun. The moon's light goes through different stages. The new moon is the first stage. You can hardly see the moon's crescent at this stage. The moon is full when it is round and very bright.

In ancient Israel, a new moon marked the beginning of a month. The Israelites held a new moon festival at this time. They would present offerings to God. Later, God did not want the offerings because the people were not obeying him.

Christians do not observe a new moon festival. They believe that Jesus became the new offering when he gave his life to save us.

Jesus is the Light of the World. **We get his light when we obey him and share his teachings.**

Name _____   Date _____

Handwriting
Trace and write.

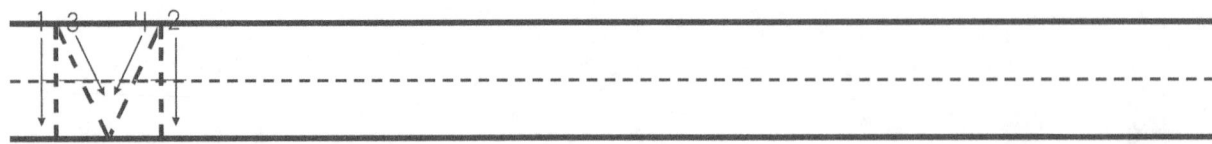

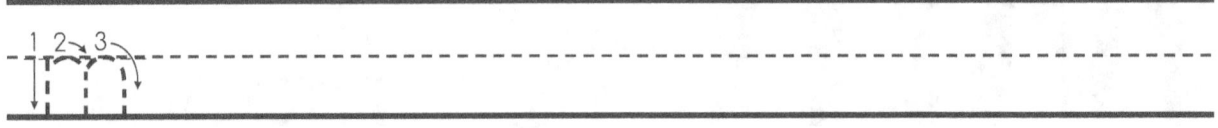

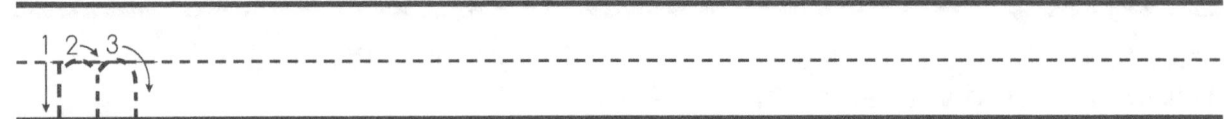

Spelling
Say the name of each picture. Then write the missing letters to complete the words.

___ug   ca___el   dru___

Identifying Sounds
Say the name of each picture. Then circle those that **begin** with the sound /m/.

The /d/ Sound

Say the picture name. Listen for the **first** letter sound. Say the sound.

Dd  donkey

Story Time: Listen carefully as your teacher or parent reads the Bible story below. What did you learn from the story?

Bible Story: The Dazed Donkey
Bible Lesson: Numbers 22:1-33
Bible Theme: Obey God

King Balak of Moab was very afraid of the Israelites. He asked Balaam to curse them. But God told Balaam not to curse the Israelites, as they are blessed.

Early one morning, Balaam got on his donkey and left to curse the Israelites. God sent an angel in the donkey's way to stop Balaam. He did not see the angel, but the donkey did. It tried to turn away, but the animal could not go left or right. The donkey fell on the dusty road. Balaam was angry, so he beat the donkey with a stick. Suddenly, God opened the donkey's mouth and it spoke.

"Master, what have I done that you should hit me three times?" the animal asked.

"You made me look like a fool," replied Balaam. "If I had a sword, I would kill you."

"Master, haven't I always been good to you?" asked the donkey. "Have I ever done this before?" God opened Balaam's eyes and he saw the angel. The angel told Balaam, that the donkey saved his life. He said he would have killed Balaam if the donkey did not stop. **We must always obey God and treat animals well.**

Handwriting
Trace and write.

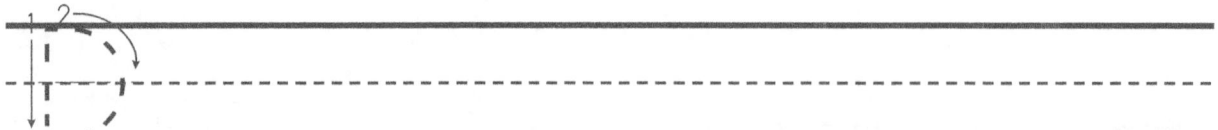

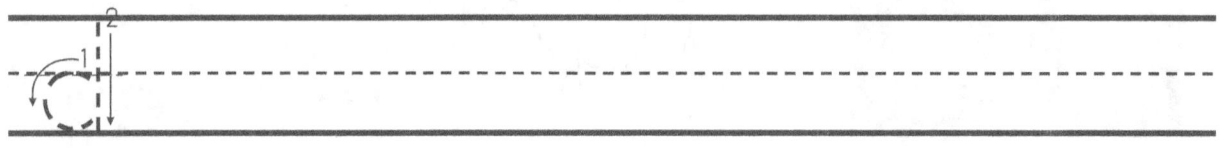

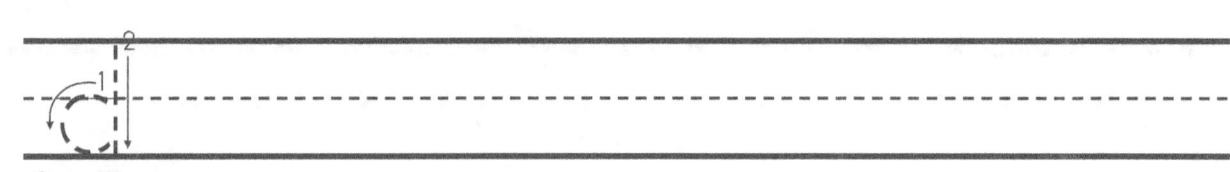

Spelling
Say the name of each picture. Then write the missing letters to complete the words.

__oll   win__ow   be__

Identifying Sounds
Say the name of each picture. Then circle those that **begin** with the sound /d/.

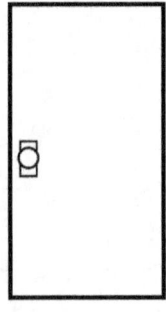      

Name _____   Date _____

High Frequency Word

Read
Say the word.

Write
Write the word.

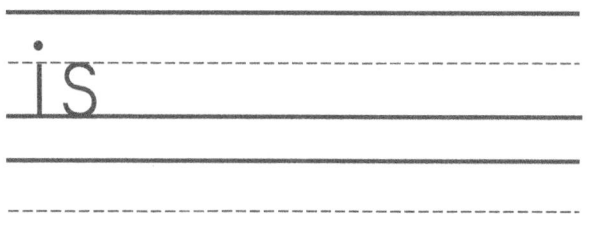

Spell
Circle the correct spelling of the word.

is   a s   is   his

Trace the word 'is' to complete the sentences. Read the sentences.

Color the word. Then write it in your word bank book.

© Quail Publishers LLC 2023   Bible Phonics Workbook 1 | 27

Name _____   Date _____

High Frequency Word

Read it
Say the word.

as

Write it
Write the word.

as

Spell it
Circle the correct spelling of the word.

is   as   has   as

Trace the word 'as' to complete the sentence. Read the sentence.

Mom is as tan as Dad.

Color the word. Then write it in your word bank book.

as

Name _____ Date _____

Blending
Use sound talk to say the letter sounds in each word. Then blend the sounds to read the words.

pin tin tam

dam nap dad

Spelling
Say the picture names. Then circle the correct spelling for each picture.

 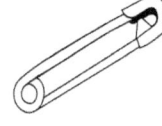 

mad mat   pin tin   tam dam

Reading
Read the sentence based on Genesis 37:23-24.

A sad man is in a pit.

Name _____ Date _____

The /g/ Sound

Say the picture name. Listen for the **first** sound. Say the first letter sound. It is the hard 'g' sound.

Gg
goat

Story Time: Listen carefully as your teacher or parent reads the Bible story below. What did you learn from the story?

Bible Story: Gruff Goats
Bible Lesson: Matthew 25: 31-41
Bible Theme: Follow Jesus

Jesus told many parables when he taught people. Parables are short stories that have good lessons. Parables help us to understand Jesus' teachings.

In one parable, Jesus said he will return to gather his people. Jesus said that he would separate the sheep from the goat.

Good people are called sheep because they obey Jesus. The sheep will gather at the right. Jesus said the sheep will live with him forever. People who do not obey Jesus are called goats. These gruff goats will gather at the left.

Jesus will tell them, "Get away from me! Go into the fire that I have made for the devil and his angels! I was hungry, and you did not feed me." He will punish these people. **This parable reminds us that we must always follow Jesus.**

Name _____   Date _____

Handwriting
Trace and write.

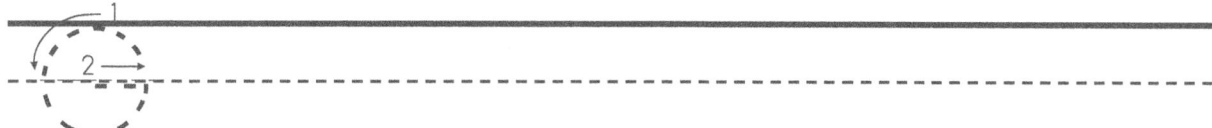

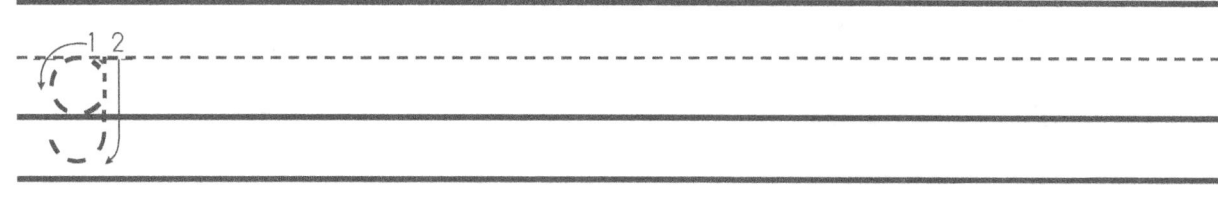

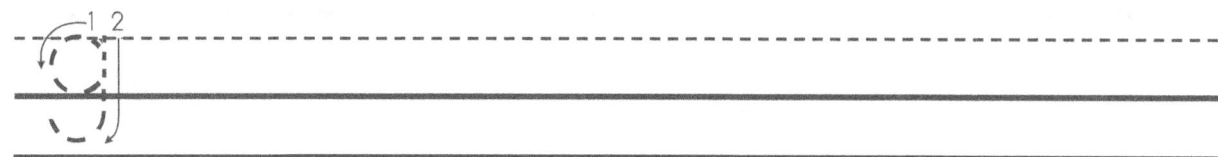

Spelling
Say the name of each picture. Then write the missing letters to complete the words.

___ate   ti___er   ba___

Identifying Sounds
Say the name of each picture. Then circle those that **begin** with the sound /g/.

The /ŏ/ Sound

Say the picture name. Listen for the **first** letter sound. Say the sound. It is the short 'o' sound.

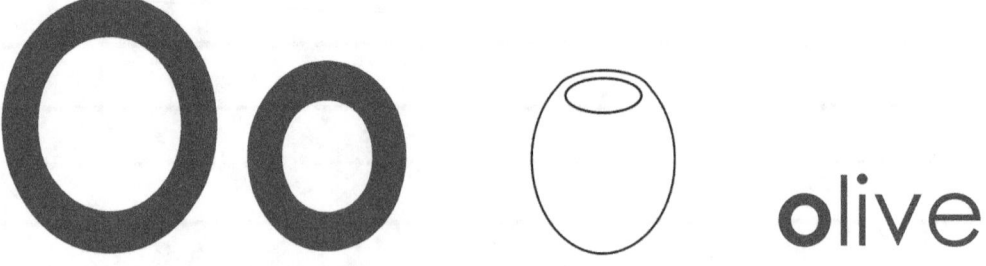 olive

Story Time: Listen carefully as your teacher or parent reads the Bible story below. What did you learn from the story?

Bible Story: Olive Oil
Bible Lesson: Exodus 27:20-21, 1 Samuel 16:13
Bible Theme: Do Good Things for Others

An olive is a small fruit that grows on olive trees. Many people use olives to make tasty dishes. They also use the fat from olives to make oil.

Olive oil was very special and holy to the Israelites. The Israelites also used olive oil as fuel for their lamps. God told Moses to tell the Israelites to bring olive oil for the lamps in the temple. He said Aaron should keep the lamps burning from evening until morning.

The Israelites also used olive oil as medicine and to anoint kings and priests. David was anointed with olive oil when he was chosen as king.

You too can be like an olive. Though small, you can do many good things for people.

Name _____   Date _____

Handwriting
Trace and write.

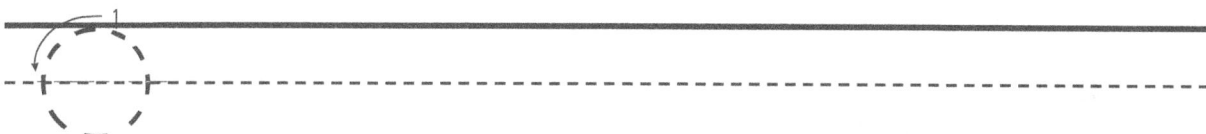

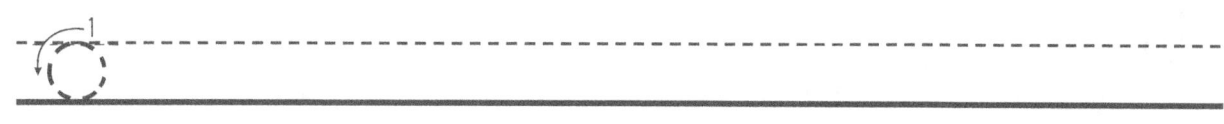

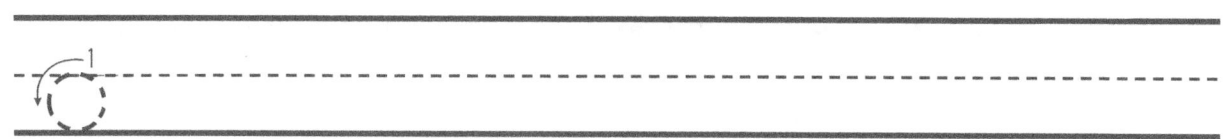

Spelling
Say the name of each picture. Then write the missing letters to complete the words.

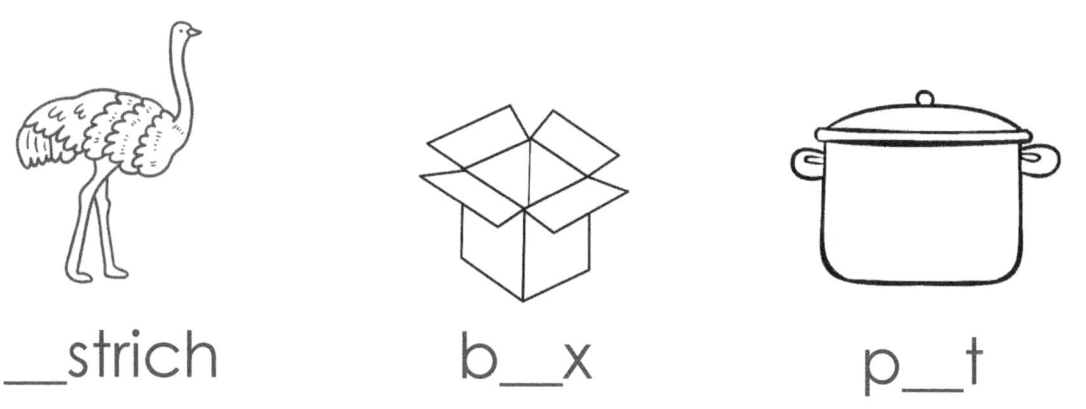

__strich   b__x   p__t

Identifying Sounds
Say the name of each picture. Then circle those that **begin** with the sound /ŏ/.

The /c/ Sound

Say the picture name. Listen for the <u>first</u> letter sound. Say the sound. It is the hard 'c' sound.

camel

Story Time: Listen carefully as your teacher or parent reads the Bible story below. What did you learn from the story?

Bible Story: A Caravan of Camels in Canaan
Bible Lesson: Genesis 24: 1-67
Bible Theme: God Answers Prayers

One day a caravan of camels with a beautiful lady arrived in Canaan. The caravan came because Abraham wanted a good wife for his son Isaac.

Abraham had said to his servant, "Go to my cousins in my homeland. You will find a wife for my son there." The servant prayed then set off with ten camels.

One evening he stopped by a well. Many women would come to the well at that time. The servant prayed that one would become the wife of Isaac. Shortly after, a lady came by.

"May I have some water please?" he said. The lady gave the servant and his camels, water.

The servant asked, "Whose daughter are you?" The lady told him that her name was Rebekah. She was Abraham's cousin.

Rebekah invited the servant to meet her family. The servant told Rebekah's family why he came. Rebekah's parents asked her if she would marry Isaac. Rebekah said yes, even though she had never met him. The servant was happy that **God had answered his prayers.**

Name _____   Date _____

Handwriting
Trace and write.

Spelling
Say the name of each picture. Then write the missing letters to complete the words.

___ ow   ___arrot   garli___

Identifying Sounds
Say the name of each picture. Then circle those that **begin** with the sound /c/.

Bible Phonics Workbook 1 | 35

Name _____   Date _____

The /k/ Sound
Say the picture name. Listen for the **first** letter sound. Say the sound.

Kk key

Story Time: Listen carefully as your teacher or parent reads the Bible story below. What did you learn from the story?

Bible Story: Keys to the Kingdom
Bible Lesson: Matthew 16: 13-19
Bible Theme: Share Your Faith

One day when Jesus was in Phillipi, he asked his disciples, "Who do people say I, the Son of Man, am?"

His disciples answered, "People say you are John the Baptist. Some people say you are Elijah. Others say you are Jeremiah or a prophet."

Jesus said, "But what about you all? Who do you say I am?"

Peter replied, "You are the Messiah, the Son of God." Jesus was very happy to hear this.

Jesus told Peter that he was blessed. He said, "You are Peter, and on this rock, I will build my church. And the gates of hell cannot stop it."

Jesus also said to Peter, "I give you the keys to the kingdom of heaven."

Keys are very special tools. They can open many doors and close them too. Peter taught many people about Christ. In this way, he opened the doors to let them know about Jesus. **We must always tell others about Jesus.**

Name _____   Date _____

Handwriting
Trace and write.

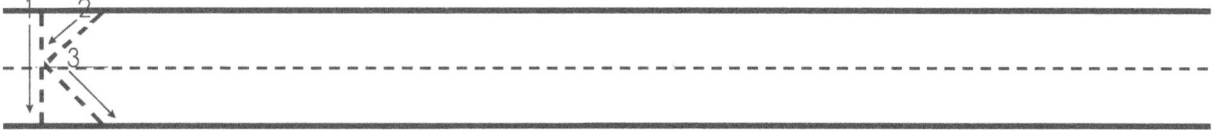

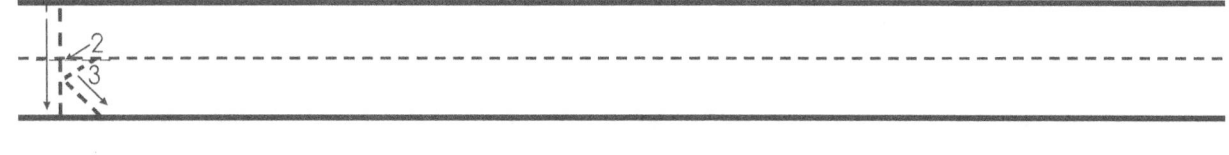

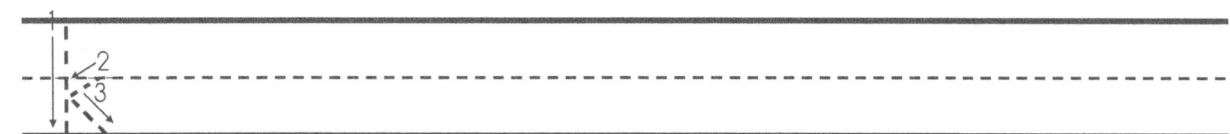

Spelling
Say the name of each picture. Then write the missing letters to complete the words.

__ite   don__ey   boo__

Identifying Sounds
Say the name of each picture. Then circle those that **begin** with the sound /k/.

Name _____   Date _____

Blending
Use sound talk to say the letter sounds in each word. Then blend the sounds to read the words.

kit   not   God

cat   got   tag

Spelling
Say the picture names. Then circle the correct spelling for each picture.

pig dig   cap tap   mop map

Reading
Read the sentence.

Kim is on a mat.

Name _____   Date _____

The /k/ Sound

Say the picture name. Listen for the **last** letter sound. Say the sound. The letters '**ck**' stand for one sound, /k/ as in sa**ck**.

 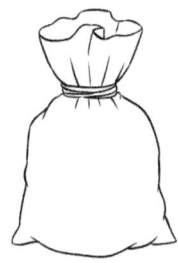 sa**ck**

Phonics Tip: When the sound /k/ is heard after a short vowel sound in a one-syllable word, it is spelled with the letters '**ck**'. For example: sa**ck**.

Blending
Use sound talk to say the letter sounds in each word. Then blend the sounds to read the words. How many sounds are in each word?

tack   sick   dock

pick   pack   sock

Reading
Read the sentence based on Luke 5:17-25.

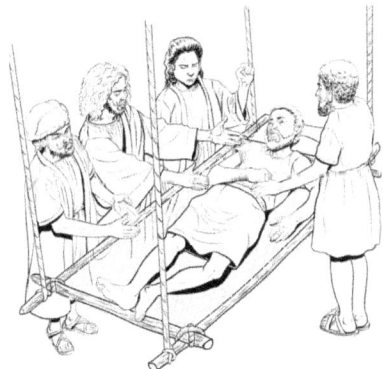

A sick man is on a cot.

Name _____ Date _____

High Frequency Word

When capital or uppercase 'I' is alone in a sentence, we say its long sound. It is also the letter name.

Read it
Say the word.

I

Write it
Write the word.

I

Trace the word 'I' to complete the sentences. Read the sentences.

I am a kid. I am not a cat.

Write it: Write the word 'I' to complete the sentence. Read the sentence. Draw or paste a picture of yourself.

___ a m _____.
                    Write your name.

Color the word. Then write it in your word bank book.

I

Name _____   Date _____

Reviewing Sounds

Beginning Sounds: Say the name of each picture. Listen carefully for the <u>first</u> sound. Circle the letter that stands for the sound.

s t p   t p n   c m p

Middle Sounds: Say the name of each picture. Listen carefully for the <u>middle</u> sound. Circle the letter that stands for the sound.

a o i   o i a   o i a

End Sounds: Say the name of each picture. Listen carefully for the <u>last</u> sound. Circle the letter that stands for the sound.

m d g   s t p   k m d

Name _____   Date _____

Rhymes
Connect the Rhymes: Read the words below. Draw a line to connect those that rhyme.

sat   dim
God   top
Kim   nod
cap   pat
mop   gap

Find the rhymes: Write the word from the box that rhymes with each underlined word to complete the captions.

| mat   tin |
| man   cop |

A <u>cat</u> on a _____.

A <u>tan</u> _____.

A <u>top</u> _____.

A <u>pin</u> in a _____.

Name _____   Date _____

Word Building with Vowels: Add vowels to complete the words. Read the new words you made. Use them in sentences.

Add 'a'	Add 'i'	Add 'o'
s__t	p__g	c__p
c__p	s__t	G__d
p__ck	k__ck	c__d
d__m	t__n	m__ck

Word Families: Read the words, then place them under the correct word family.

sat	sip	tip	mock	dip
mat	sock		cat	dock

-at words   **-ip words**   **ock words**

_____   _____   _____

_____   _____   _____

_____   _____   _____

Name _____   Date _____

Steps to Spelling

- **Look** carefully at each picture.
- **Say** the picture name.
- **Listen** for the letter sounds.
- **Write** the letters that represent the sounds. Use the sound buttons (•) to guide you. Each stands for **one** sound. A sound button below a long line (⎯•⎯) represents a digraph (two letters that stand for one sound).
- **Read** the word that you have written.
- **Check** your spelling.

___ ___ ___   ___ ___ ___   ___ ___ ___
 •   •   •   •   •   •   •   •   •

      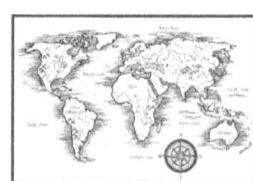

___ ___ ___   ___ ___ ___   ___ ___ ___
 •   •   •   •   •   •   •   •   •

Guess the Riddles: Listen carefully as your teacher, or parent, reads the riddles below. Then write the missing letters to complete the word.

The creator of the world.   G ___ ___

You wipe your feet on it.   m ___ ___

An animal that barks, "wuff, wuff".   d ___ ___

You cook in it.   p ___ ___

44 © Quail Publishers LLC 2023   Bible Phonics Workbook 1

Spelling: Write the picture names on the lines then read the sentences.

It is a _____.

It is a _____.

It is a _____.

It is a _____.

It is a _____.

It is a _____.

It is a _____.

It is a _____.

Name _____   Date _____

High Frequency Word

Read the captions with the word, '**and**'. Write a sentence with the word. Make sure that you follow the checklist.

God **and** man.

Cats **and** dogs.

Mom **and** Dad.

Tim **and** Kim.

Capital Letter	Spelling	Handwriting	Finger spaces	Punctuation	Sentence Makes Sense
A	and	✍	👆	•	🙂

Name _____   Date _____

The Alphabet
Every letter has a position in the alphabet. Write the missing letters of the alphabet in their upper and lowercase forms.

____   Bb   ____   ____   Ee

Ff   ____   Hh   ____   Jj

____   Ll   ____   ____   ____

____   Qq   Rr   ____   ____

Uu   Vv   Ww   Xx   Yy

Zz

Letter Shapes
Match each uppercase letter with its lowercase form

S	t		M	g
A	n		D	k
T	i		G	d
P	s		O	c
I	a		C	o
N	p		K	m

© Quail Publishers LLC 2023   Bible Phonics Workbook 1

Name _____ Date _____

Comprehension: Read the passage and answer the questions.

Ants in Pants

Ants! Ants!
Ants in a pan.
Ants on a can.
Ants on a pip
Ants on Nip.
Ants on Dad.
Dad is mad.
Ants! Ants!
Ants in pants!

Write the correct word on the line to complete each sentence. Then write the word pairs that rhyme in your notebooks.

1. Ants on a _____.
   a. can   b. pin   d. fan

2. Dad is _____.
   a. sip   b. mad   c. tip

3. An ant is in _____.
   a. picks   b. pats   c. pants

Discussion
1. Ants are insects. Can you name some other insects?
2. How many legs does an insect have? Count the legs of an ant to find out.
3. What does the Bible say about ants?

Name _____   Date _____

Building Sentences: Read the sentence based on Luke 2:16.

A tot is in a cot.

Write a sentence about the picture. Make sure that you follow your checklist.

Capital Letter	Spelling	Handwriting	Finger spaces	Punctuation	Sentence Makes Sense
A	sat	✋	☝	•	🙁

© Quail Publishers LLC 2023

Name _____ Date _____

Reading: Read the following sentences.

Tod got a dog and cat.

Mom is not as sick as Dad.

I am not sick.

Kim can not sit on a mat.

A pin is on a map.

A sick man is on a mat.

Tim did not nod.

A dog is on a mat.

It is not Tim. It is Sam.

Kit and Nip dig and dig.

Name _____   Date _____

Numbers and Number Names. These are some numbers and number names that you must learn. Some of the words do not follow the spelling rules. Learn how to spell them.

Read it Say the name of the numbers.	Write it Trace the numbers and number names.	Spell it Write the number names.
1	1 one	
2	2 two	
3	3 three	
4	4 four	
5	5 five	
6	6 six	
7	7 seven	
8	8 eight	
9	9 nine	
10	10 ten	

Word List Below is a list of words with the letters and sounds taught in this workbook. The list also includes high frequency words. Read the words, then use them to build sentences.

Letter Sets	Words			
1 s a t p	s	a	+t	+p
High Frequency a at		a	at sat	pat sap tap
2 i n m d	+i	+n	+m	+d
High Frequency it in am dad did *is *as	it sit pit pip tip sip	nip nap an pan man Nan tan in pin sin tin	am tam Sam Pam mat man map mam	dad sad pad mad did dim dam din dip
3 g o c k	+g	+o	+c	+k
High Frequency on not can mom *I	tag gag nag sag gig pig dig gas gap	on pot not dot got pop top sop mop dog sog God mom	cod cob cop cot con cat cap can	kit kin kid Kim
	+ck	**Simple words with two syllables**		
	kick tick pick sick Nick Dick sock mock dock sack tack pack	nap/kin = napkin pic/nic = picnic pan/da = panda mom/ma = momma		

Letter Tiles: Copy the letter tiles onto card stock paper. Cut them out and have children use them to spell words as they learn the letter sounds.

s	a	t
p	i	n
m	d	g
o	c	k

Letter Tiles: Copy the letter tiles onto card stock paper. Cut them out and have children use them to spell words as they learn the letter sounds.

ck	e	u
r	h	b
f	ff	l
ll	ss	j

Letter Tiles: Copy the letter tiles onto card stock paper. Cut them out and have children use them to spell words as they learn the letter sounds.

v	w	x
y	z	zz
qu	ch	tch
sh	th	ng

Letter Tiles: Copy the letter tiles onto card stock paper. Cut them out and have children use them to spell words as they learn the letter sounds.

nk	wh	A
E	I	O
U	a	e
i	o	u